Around the House with Mot

A Guide to Using Nursery Rhymes to Explore Multiple Intelligences

Written by Carol Lemoine

Illustrated by Becky J. Radtke

Fearon Teacher Aids
A Division of Frank Schaffer Publications, Inc.

*This is dedicated to anyone and everyone who appreciates the wisdom
and enjoys the whimsy of Mother Goose nursery rhymes!*

Editors: Kim Cernek, Kristin Eclov, Christine Hood
Cover Illustration: Becky J. Radtke
Book Design: Good Neighbor Press, Inc.

Fearon Teacher Aids products were formerly manufactured and distributed by American Teaching Aids, Inc., a subsidiary of Silver Burdett Ginn, and are now manufactured and distributed by Frank Schaffer Publications, Inc. FEARON, FEARON TEACHER AIDS, and the FEARON balloon logo are marks used under license from Simon & Schuster, Inc.

© **Fearon Teacher Aids**
A Division of Frank Schaffer Publications, Inc.
23740 Hawthorne Boulevard
Torrance, CA 90505-5927

FE211010

Table of Contents

© Fearon Teacher Aids FE211010

Welcoming Words

The Nature of Nursery Rhymes

Welcome to the world of wisdom and whimsy! *Around the House with Mother Goose* is a guide for kindergarten and first-grade teachers who are interested in using nursery rhymes to explore their students' multiple intelligences.

A form of folk art, a nursery rhyme is a short, amusing verse which tells an anecdote or riddle, satirizes a political or social event, lulls a baby to sleep, accompanies a game, or teaches children about the alphabet and counting. Many of the original authors of nursery rhymes are unknown. And, since these verses have been passed down through an oral tradition, there are often many versions of the same rhyme.

The Meaning of Multiple Intelligences

The nursery rhymes of Mother Goose are so familiar to children and adults that they are the perfect vehicle for implementing Howard Gardner's theory of multiple intelligences (*Frames of Mind: The Theory of Multiple Intelligences* by Howard Gardner, Basic Books, Inc., Publishers, 1993). Gardner proposes that everyone possesses multiple intelligences that are relatively independent of each other. These nine intelligences are labeled as follows: *bodily-kinesthetic, interpersonal, intrapersonal, linguistic, logical-mathematical, musical, spatial, naturalist,* and *existentialist.* An individual might favor one intelligence over another, although Gardner suggests that most people can develop adequate levels of competency in each. Gardner's list of multiple intelligences is not finite. It keeps changing with each new addition. In this book, we will not be addressing the specifics of the latest addition to Gardner's multiple intelligences—existentialist. Two recommended resources for using the multiple intelligences in K–1 classrooms are *Multiple Intelligences: Teaching Kids the Way They Learn*, Grade Kindergarten (FS23279) and *Multiple Intelligences: Teaching Kids the Way They Learn*, Grade 1 (FS23280), Frank Schaffer Publications, Inc., 1999.

Exploring Multiple Intelligences Through Nursery Rhymes

Nursery rhymes provide fun, safe, and inviting opportunities for students to explore each intelligence. The chart on page 7 identifies and defines all nine areas. Related concepts and recommended activities for each are also included.

While some children may demonstrate a strength in a particular area, it is more likely that their nine intelligences are overlapped and intertwined. Although a child's previous experiences, knowledge, feelings, and environmental factors also contribute to his or her progress as a student, the ability to recognize the dominant intelligences of your

© Fearon Teacher Aids FE211010

students allows you to find new and creative avenues for enhancing learning in your classroom.

Exploring multiple intelligences through nursery rhymes is an especially effective approach for teachers of emergent and beginning readers. Educators of primary students recognize that phonemic awareness and familiarity with rhymes are essential for students to become successful readers.

Optimize the usefulness of this resource by analyzing the dynamics of your class. Use the Observational Study for Multiple Intelligences survey on page 8 to examine each child's strengths and weaknesses. Then, take the survey yourself. As you analyze the data, you might find that the student who seems hardest to reach is the child who is strongest in your weakest intelligence.

Around the House with Mother Goose

This resource provides creative, hands-on activities that are easy to implement and assess. Mother Goose will lead students to many different places where they will meet many familiar faces. Each of eleven nursery rhymes includes the following:

- A **verse** to reproduce and have students color and use for reference during the activities. Suggested uses for the verse include: choral reading, sight-word identification, rhyming-word identification, and playing games.

- An original, hands-on **activity** for each of the eight intelligences represented in this book. Some activities may address more than one intelligence.

- Materials lists that clearly identify the things you will need to implement each activity.

- **Reproducible patterns** that complement each theme.

- **Student-activity pages** that extend the learning for many activities.

Tell children to fasten their seatbelts because, with the help of Mother Goose, they are really going places!

The Nine Intelligences

Intelligence	Definition	Ability/Concept	Activities/Experiences
Bodily-Kinesthetic	Whole body and hands	To control body motions and handle objects	Hands-on, active learning
Interpersonal	Social understanding	To notice and make distinctions among individual moods, temperaments, motivations, and intentions	Social, group activities
Intrapersonal	Self-knowledge	To access own feelings, thoughts, emotions, and intuitions	Independent, private activities
Linguistic	Words	To use language through reading and writing	Crossword puzzles, creating stories
Logical-Mathematical	Numbers and reasoning	To manipulate, order, and assess quantity and quality	Logical puzzles, strategy games, patterns, categories, and relationships
Musical	Tone, rhythm, and timbre	To think in melodic and harmonious sounds	Singing, producing music
Spatial	Pictures and images	To focus on physical attributes of one's surroundings	Jigsaw puzzles, mazes, painting, sculpting
Naturalist	Appreciates the natural world	To understand and appreciate the natural world	Caring for plants and animals, classifying shells, insects, and rocks
Existentialist	Recognizes the "big picture"	To understand how humankind fits into the "big picture"	May not be applicable at this stage of development

© Fearon Teacher Aids FE211010

Observational Study for Multiple Intelligences

Place a checkmark beside each activity the student generally appears to prefer to make an informal assessment of the intelligences he or she naturally exercises.

Name _____   Date _____

Bodily-Kinesthetic

_____ dance/exercise
_____ physical games
_____ role play/drama
_____ manipulatives

Linguistic

_____ crossword puzzles
_____ word games
_____ poetry
_____ storytelling/writing

Spatial

_____ visually stimulated
_____ mazes/puzzles
_____ compares/contrasts
_____ diagrams

Interpersonal

_____ cooperative group work
_____ board games
_____ discussions
_____ puppet shows

Logical-Mathematical

_____ brain teasers
_____ strategy games
_____ numbers
_____ classification

Naturalist

_____ caring for plants/animals
_____ collecting seashells
_____ classifying insects/habitats
_____ creating classroom habitats

Intrapersonal

_____ critiques own work
_____ feels attuned to self
_____ works individually
_____ silent reading

Musical

_____ creates own songs
_____ produces melodies
_____ prefers harmony
_____ recognizes rhythm

Notes:
_____
_____
_____
_____
_____
_____
_____
_____

8

© Fearon Teacher Aids FE211010

There Was an Old Woman

There was an old woman
Who lived in a shoe.
She had so many children
She didn't know what to do.
She gave them some broth
Without any bread.
She kissed them all soundly
And sent them to bed.

© Fearon Teacher Aids FE211010

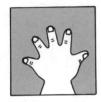

Shoe Scramble

Materials

shoes

Mother Goose in the closet.

Lead students to a gym, field, or other open area. Invite students to remove their shoes, and have them place them in a pile in the center of the playing area. Give each student a number. Have all students with an even number line up on one side of the play area and all students with an odd number line up on the other side. Call one even and one odd number. Tell the two students with those numbers to race to the center of the circle, find their shoes, place them on their feet, and return to their team. The first person to do this earns a point for her or his team. Continue until each student has retrieved her or his shoes. The team with the most points wins.

If the Shoe Fits

Materials

Shoe activity page (page 14)
magazines
scissors
glue
pencils
stapler

The person wearing these shoes is a construction worker.

Invite students to look through magazines for pictures of people wearing shoes. Have students cut out pictures of people doing jobs that require special shoes. Give each student a Shoe activity page and have him or her cut out the shoe. Have students glue their magazine picture to one side of the shoe and write about what the person wearing this shoe does. Collect students' work, and staple their shoe cutouts together under another shoe titled *If the Shoe Fits*.

How Many Shoes Are You?

Materials

Shoe Measurements activity page (page 15)
Shoe activity page (page 14)
pencils

Give each student a copy of the Shoe Measurements activity page and the Shoe activity page, and have him or her cut out the shoe. Invite students to use their shoe cutouts to measure: the length of their desks, the length of a table, the width of the door, the distance across the room, and themselves. Have students record their information on the Shoe Measurements activity page. Challenge students to find an item in the room that is the same length as their shoe cutout, and have them record the name of the object at the bottom of the reproducible.

Famous Pairs

Materials

Shoe activity page (page 14)
scissors
marker

Make one copy of the Shoe activity page for each student. (If there is not an even number of students, give one student two shoes.) Ask students to cut out the shoes. Write or draw a picture of one part of a familiar pair of people or objects on each shoe. If appropriate, include pictures and words on the shoe cutouts. For example, write the following on ten different shoes: *peanut butter, jelly, salt, pepper, Jack, Jill, left, right, cookie,* and *milk.* Mix up the shoe cutouts in a pile. Have students sit in a circle, and give each one a shoe cutout. Ask one student to stand and read the word on her or his cutout. Encourage the student with the matching word to stand and read her or his word. For example, a student reads the word *ice cream,* and the student with the word *cone* stands and reads. Play until each shoe finds its match.

11

Siblings Graph

Materials

Graph activity page (page 16)
index cards
pencils
chalkboard/chalk
tape
crayons or markers

Give each student an index card on which to write his or her name. Write *0, 1, 2, 3,* and so on, along the bottom of the chalkboard. Invite students to tape their cards above the number that describes how many sisters or brothers they have. Distribute a copy of the Graph activity page to each student. Have students color the boxes that represent the number of siblings of each student. Ask students questions such as: *Do more students have one sibling or two siblings? If the whole class and their siblings belonged to Mother Goose, how many children would that be?*

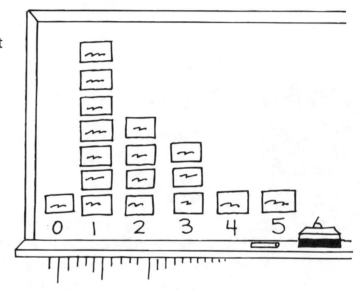

Footloose

Materials

Invite students to think of different ways they can use their feet to create a rhythm for "There Was an Old Woman." Have students tap their feet, hop, or jump as they chant the verse. Encourage students to experiment with the tempo and volume of the rhythms they create.

Footprints

Materials
Shoe activity page (page 14)
scissors
hole punch
yarn or string

Distribute two copies of the Shoe activity page to each student. Have students cut out each shoe. Use a hole punch to create five or six matching holes on both shoe cutouts. Have students use string or yarn to lace the two shoe cutouts together. Encourage students to use their "shoe books" to write stories about their favorite pairs of shoes.

Feet Match

Materials
copy paper
crayons
scissors

Divide the class into pairs. Give each pair two sheets of paper and crayons. Have children take off their shoes and trace around their partner's feet. Then cut out the paper feet. Remind children to write their names on the back of their feet patterns. Invite each pair of children to mix up their paper feet and then try to match them up again. Encourage children to look closely at their own feet to help them find their matching paper feet. If appropriate, invite two pairs to mix and match their feet patterns.

Shoe

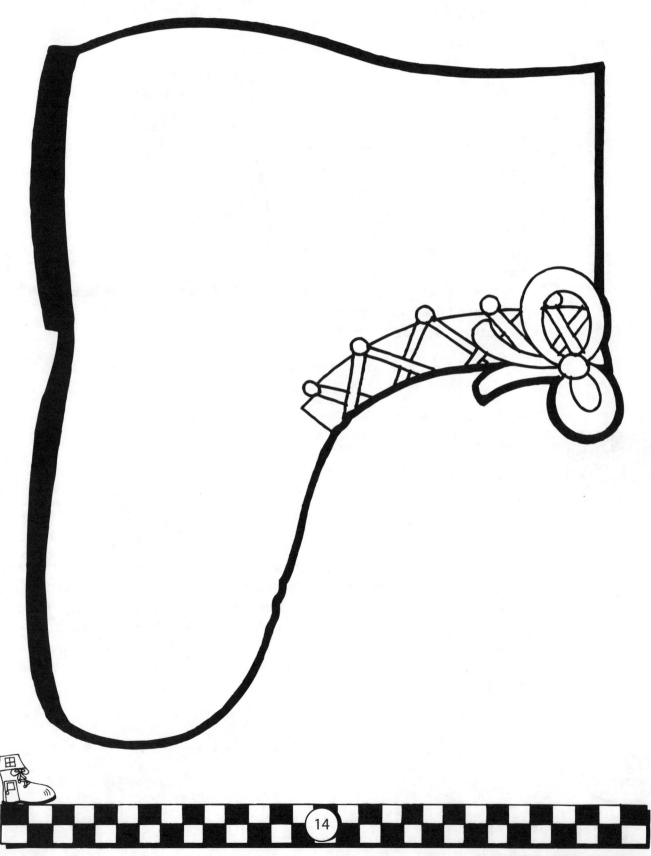

© Fearon Teacher Aids FE211010

Name _____

Shoe Measurements

Object	How Many Shoes?
desk	
table	
door	
room	
me	

What is the same length as the shoe?

_____

- -

_____

15

Name _____

_____ **Graph**

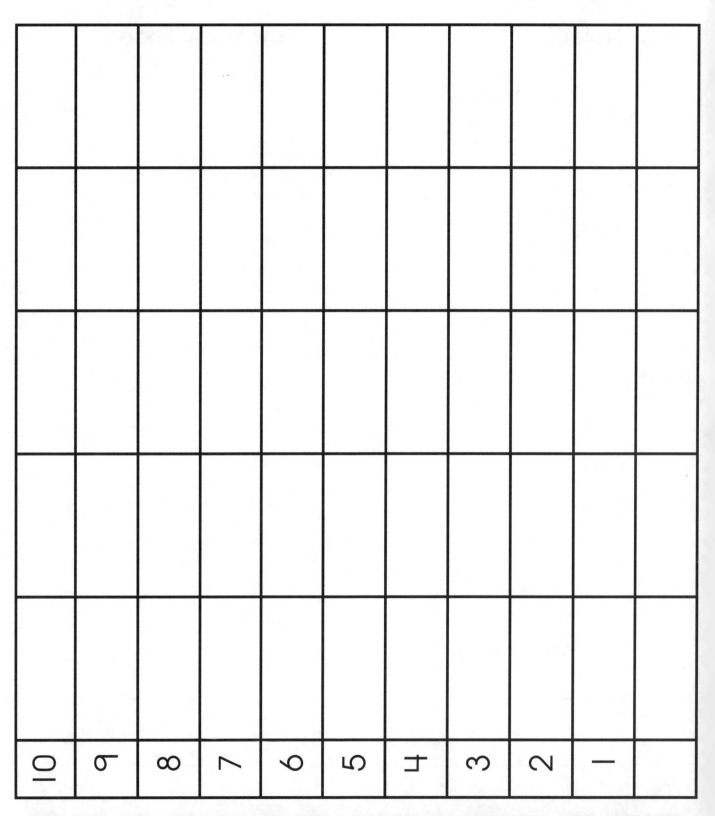

| 10 | 9 | 8 | 7 | 6 | 5 | 4 | 3 | 2 | 1 | |

reproducible

Little Miss Muffet

Little Miss Muffet
Sat on a tuffet,
Eating her curds and whey;
Along came a spider,
And sat down beside her,
And frightened Miss Muffet away.

reproducible

⋅ Little Miss Muffet ⋅

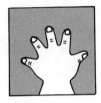

Paper Bag Puppets

Materials
Miss Muffet activity page (page 22)
Spider activity page (page 23)
crayons or markers
scissors
glue
brown paper lunch bags

Give each child a copy of the Miss Muffet and Spider activity pages, and two brown paper lunch bags. Invite children to color the Miss Muffet and spider figures. Tell them to cut out the puppets and glue each to the side of an open paper bag. Invite children to retell "Little Miss Muffet" using their puppets.

Mother Goose in the attic.

Who's Sitting Where?

Materials
sentence strips
marker
pocket chart
drawing paper
crayons or colored pencils

Write each word of the first two lines of "Little Miss Muffet" on a different sentence strip, but use a different-colored sentence strip for the underlined words: *Little Miss Muffet*/*Sat on a tuffet*. Place the strips in a pocket chart, and invite students to read the sentences aloud. Encourage children to change the underlined words to give Miss Muffet a new name and place to sit. Remind students that the new words must rhyme. For example, students might change the lines to: *Little Miss Mair/Sat on a chair*, or *Little Miss Mane/Sat on a plane*. Encourage students to illustrate these images on paper, and bind them together into a class book titled *Who's Sitting Where?*

18

What Frightened You Away?

Materials
Spider activity page (page 23)
Writing Lines activity page (page 24)
scissors
crayons or colored pencils
pencils
black marker

Make one copy of the Spider and Writing Lines activity pages. Cut out the spider and trace the outline over the writing lines using a black marker. Make one copy of the lined spider for each student to cut out. Invite students to think about something that frightens them, and then draw a picture of this fear on the blank side of the spider. Ask students to write or dictate their ideas on the lines on the back of the spider. Encourage children to read their stories to partners.

Sounds from a Spider

Materials
Spider activity page (page 23)
scissors
crayons or markers

Give each student or pairs of students a copy of the Spider activity page to cut out. Ask students to write a letter of the alphabet on the front of their spider cutout and a word or picture that begins with that letter on the back. For example, *d* and *dog*. Invite individual or pairs of students to stand before the class and show the side of the spider cutouts with the letters. Teach the class the following version of "Little Miss Muffet":

> *Little Miss Muffet*
> *Sat on a tuffet*
> *Eating her curds and whey.*
> *Along came a spider*
> *And sat down beside her*
> *And gave her a* d *word to say.*

Ask each student to turn over his or her spider to reveal the word or picture. Ask the class to repeat the word. Invite a new student or pair of students to share their letters and words. Change the verse to include the new letter, and have the class chant the rhyme again.

19

Making Eight

Materials
Spider activity page (page 23)
scissors
crayons or markers
pencils

Distribute a copy of the Spider activity page to each student. Ask them to cut out the spider and then count the spider's legs. Encourage students to use one color crayon or marker to color some of the legs and another color to color the remaining legs. Show students how to write an equation for this on the spider's body. For example, a student who colored three legs red and five legs blue would write $3 + 5 = 8$ on the spider's body. Ask students to turn over their spiders and repeat the activity.

Along Came a . . .

Materials
chalk/chalkboard

Invite students to change the name of the creature that visits Miss Muffet. Write the following version of "Little Miss Muffet" on the board. Encourage children to create a melody and actions for the new verses. For example, students could flap their arms and sing:

Little Miss Muffet
Sat on a tuffet
Eating her curds and whey.
A <u>bird</u> came along,
And sang her this song.
So she decided to stay.

Invite students to change the underlined word to name Miss Muffet's new visitor.

Space for Spiders

Materials
Spider activity page (page 23)
scissors

Explain to students that a *tuffet* is a low seat. Make several copies of the Spider activity page available to students. Ask students to cut out the spiders. Invite students to estimate how many spider cutouts would fit along the length of their chair, the teacher's chair, their desk, the teacher's desk, and other places. Encourage students to use the spider cutouts to determine the actual number of spiders that fit in these spaces.

Spider Webs

Materials
Spider activity page (page 23)
fishing line
tape

Explain that the spider in the verse "Little Miss Muffet" swings down from his or her spider web on a silk thread called a *dragline*. The *dragline* is also referred to as the *lifeline*, because a spider often uses it to escape enemies. Spider silk is the strongest natural fiber and cannot be dissolved in water. It is produced in glands in the spider, and the spinnerets located on the spider's abdomen work like fingers to spin the silk into a web.

Give each child a copy of the Spider activity page and a piece of fishing line. Have children color and cut out the spider. Tape the fishing line to the abdomen of the spider opposite the head. Encourage children to wind up the fishing line and toss the spider while still holding onto the spider's "dragline."

© Fearon Teacher Aids FE211010

Miss Muffet

© Fearon Teacher Aids FE21101(

Name _____

Spider

23

Name _____

Writing Lines

© Fearon Teacher Aids FE211010

Old Mother Hubbard

Old Mother Hubbard
Went to the cupboard,
To give her poor dog a bone;
But when she got there
The cupboard was bare,
And so the poor dog had none.

© Fearon Teacher Aids FE211010

reproducible

Old Mother Hubbard

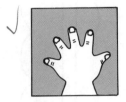

Hubbard's Cupboard Game

Materials
students' shoes

Lead the class to a large open area. Organize the class into two teams, and have them line up beside each other. (If there is not an equal number of students, have one student go twice.) Have all students that are standing behind the first two students in line remove one shoe and place it in a pile opposite where the teams are lined up. Tell the first student in each line that they are Mother/Father Hubbard, and their dog is the student in line directly behind them. Tell these students that they are going to the "cupboard" (the pile of shoes directly across from them) to find their dog a "bone" (the shoe of the student behind them). Tell the first students in line to race to find the shoes, return them to the students, and move to the back of the line. Meanwhile, the second student in line becomes the next Mother/Father Hubbard. Encourage these students to replace their shoes on their feet and race to the cupboard for the bone of the next "dog" in line.

Mother Goose in the pantry.

To Market for Mother

Materials
empty boxes and cans of grocery-
    store items
paper
scissors
tape
pencils
play money and/or play cash register

Set up a center for students to go "shopping" for groceries for Mother Hubbard. Furnish the area with empty boxes and cans of real products from a grocery store. Encourage students to play the roles of cashier, stocker, and customer by arranging the groceries, creating price tags, making grocery lists, and exchanging money.

Hubbard's Hospitality

Materials
Cupboard activity page (page 30)
scissors
glue
white construction paper
crayons or colored pencils

Tell children that they have been invited to stay as a guest at Old Mother Hubbard's house, and explain that she would like to make sure that her cupboard is not bare when they arrive. Give each student a copy of the Cupboard activity page, and have him or her write his or her name across the doors. Ask students to cut out the cupboard. Show students how to cut along the broken lines of the doors, and then glue their cupboards to construction paper. Make sure children don't glue down the doors so they can swing open. Invite students to draw pictures of their favorite foods in the space behind the doors. Display student work around the room.

Dogs, Bones, and Homophones

Materials
Dog activity page (page 31)
Bone activity page (page 32)
scissors
marker

These are not homophones in my dialect.

Copy and cut out enough pairs of Dog activity pages and Bone activity pages so that each student will receive either a dog or bone. On the dogs and bones, write pairs of homophones, such as *our/hour, two/too, poor/pour, see/sea, hear/here, so/sew,* and *bare/bear.* (For example, write *our* on a dog and *hour* on a bone.) Arrange the class so that half the students is on one side of the room and the other half is on the opposite side. Give each child in one group a dog and each person in the other group a bone. Tell students that you will call out a word and that both students holding that word should go to the middle of the room. Explain that you will say a sentence using each word. Ask the student holding the homophone that correctly fits the sentence to raise his or her word in the air. For example, say *The poor little kittens lost their mittens,* and *I will pour you a glass of lemonade.* Invite the class to clap when the correct word is raised. Repeat the activity with a new pair of homophones.

27

Mother Hubbard Math

Materials

Cupboard activity page (page 30)
scissors
stapler
marker

Make several copies of the Cupboard activity page. Cut out the cupboards and cut along the dotted lines of the doors. Staple the cupboards onto a covered bulletin board so that the doors swing open. Title the bulletin board *Mother Hubbard Math*. Write a simple addition or subtraction problem across the doors of each cupboard and the solution to each problem behind the doors. Invite students to solve the problems before they open the doors to reveal the answers.

Mother Hubbard Had a Dog

Materials

Invite students to change the words to the song "B-I-N-G-O." Have students substitute the word *Bingo* with another five-letter word. For example:

Mother Hubbard had a dog
And <u>Ringo</u> was her name-o.
R-I-N-G-O, R-I-N-G-O, R-I-N-G-O
And Ringo was her name-o.

Encourage students to use motions other than clapping their hands to signify the letters that are omitted every time the verse is sung. For example, stomping feet, jumping, or tapping pencils on desks. Change the underlined word in the verse to another five-letter word, and have students sing it again.

Still Hungry

Materials

Maze activity page (page 33)
pencils

Distribute a copy of the Maze activity page to each student. Invite students to draw the path Old Mother Hubbard's dog would follow to find each treat. Encourage students to color their pages.

What Kind of Dog?

Materials

paper
crayons
dog reference books

The nursery rhyme "Old Mother Hubbard" doesn't specify what her dog looked like, only that he or she was hungry. Encourage children to draw pictures of Old Mother Hubbard's dog. Explain that there are more than 300 kinds of purebred dogs as well as many combinations of breeds.

Give each child paper and crayons. Encourage children to look at dog reference books and then draw their favorite kinds of dog or to create their own unique dog. Invite children to share their pictures of Old Mother Hubbard's dog with the class.

Name _____

Cupboard

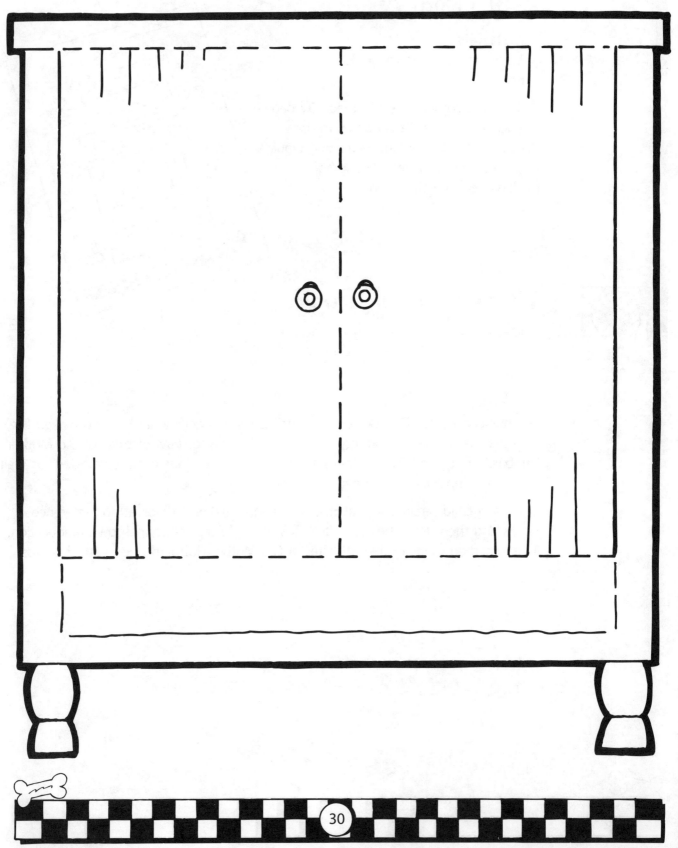

Name _____

Dog

reproducible

Name _____

Bone

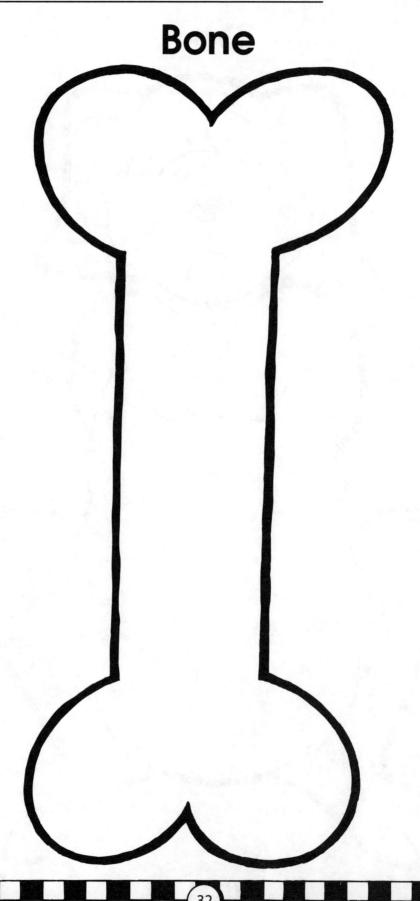

© Fearon Teacher Aids FE211010

Name _____

Maze

© Fearon Teacher Aids FE211010

Little Jack Horner

Little Jack Horner
Sat in the corner,
Eating his Christmas pie:
He put in his thumb,
And pulled out a plum,
And said, "What a good boy am I!"

© Fearon Teacher Aids FE211010

Little Jack Horner

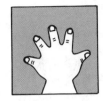

Busy Bakers

Materials
flour
salt
water
food coloring
mixing bowls
mixing spoon
measuring cups/spoons
muffin or pie tins
tempera paint
paintbrushes

Mother Goose in the dining room.

Mix together 1 cup (250 mL) flour, ½ cup (125 mL) salt, 1 cup (250 mL) water, and one to two drops food coloring for every four students. Knead dough, and divide it between four students. Invite students to form "pies" using muffin or pie tins. Allow the dough to dry over a few days, and encourage students to paint their creations to look like real pies. Invite students to use their pies to recreate the action in "Little Jack Horner."

Questions from the Corner

Materials
chart paper/marker or chalkboard/chalk
paper
pencils

Divide the class into pairs. Have students pretend to be Little Jack Horner and interview each other. Give each student a piece of paper, and show the class how to fold it into four equal parts. Encourage students to write or draw their answers to each question in one of the boxes. Print the following questions on chart paper or the chalkboard:

> *Where do you like to sit in your home?*
> *What kind of pie do you like?*
> *What is your favorite holiday?*
> *What can you do well?*

Read the first question aloud to students. Give students time to interview each other and record the answers they receive. Repeat the procedure with the remaining three questions. Invite students to share what they've learned about their classmates.

© Fearon Teacher Aids FE211010

Things for Thumbs

Materials
ink pads
paper
crayons or colored pencils
paper towels

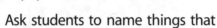

Ask students to name things that
they can do with their thumbs. Invite students to press their thumbs on an ink pad
and then on a piece of paper. Encourage them to decorate their thumbprints to look
like characters and then draw settings for the thumbprints relating to something a
thumb can do. For example, a student might draw his or her thumbprint dancing on
piano keys or digging in a garden. Display student work around the room.

Word Tree

Materials
Plum activity page (page 39)
white butcher paper
markers
scissors
tape

Cut a large sheet of white
butcher paper. To create a tree,
use a brown marker to draw a
trunk and branches and a green marker to draw leaves. Make a copy of the Plum
activity page and cut out the plum. Use the plum pattern as a template to trace
and cut out more plums from light purple construction paper. On each plum, write
a word that starts with *pl* (*plot, plant, plump, play*) or *th* (*think, they, them, that*).
Hold up a plum, and read the word to the class. Invite the class to hold their
thumbs in the air if the word starts with the *th* sound, as in *thumb*. Tape plums
with the *th* sound on the trunk of the tree. Encourage students to pretend to take a
bite out of a plum if the word starts with the *pl* sound, as in *plum*. Tape these
words onto the tree branches. If appropriate, invite students to read the *pl* words
and then the *th* words aloud.

Pie Parts

Materials

Pie activity page (page 40)
crayons or markers
scissors

Give each student or pair of students four copies of the Pie activity page. Ask students to point to the first pie. Have them divide the pie into four equal parts and then color one piece of the pie. Tell students that they colored one-fourth, or one out of four, pieces of the pie. Have students point to the second pie, and ask them to divide the pie into four sections and then color two pieces. Prompt students to say how much of the pie they colored this time. Ask students to continue the process by coloring three pieces of the third pie and four pieces of the fourth pie. After the activity, invite students to cut apart the last pie and quiz each other on the different ways to divide their pies. Encourage students to use fraction words in their discussions.

Thumb Music

Materials

twist-on metal bottle caps

Invite students to find creative ways to make music with their thumbs. Encourage students to tap their thumbs on different surfaces. Show them how to make castanets by taping twist-on metal bottle caps to their thumbs and forefingers and clicking them together. Invite students to use their thumb music to accompany a reading of "Little Jack Horner."

37

We've Got It Cornered

Materials
graph paper
crayons or colored pencils
scissors

Invite students to use graph paper to draw objects that have corners, such as a desk, book, door, or room. Then have them cut out the shapes. Encourage students to discuss what these objects have in common.

Thumbprints

Materials
ink pad
paper
magnifying glasses (one for each student pair)
paper towels

Divide the class into pairs. Explain that each person has his or her own unique thumbprint. Invite children to look at their thumbs and describe what they see. Have each student press his or her thumb into the ink pad and press it firmly onto a piece of paper. Give each pair of students a magnifying glass. Encourage them to look through the magnifying glasses and examine each unique thumbprint. Invite interested students to compare thumbprints with classmates and discuss what they see.

Name _____

Plum

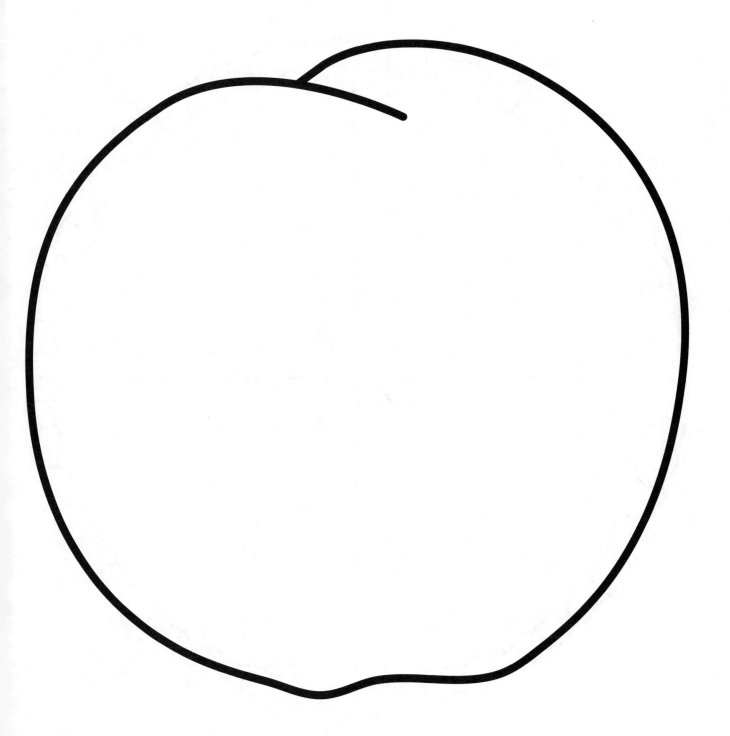

reproducible

Name _____

Pie

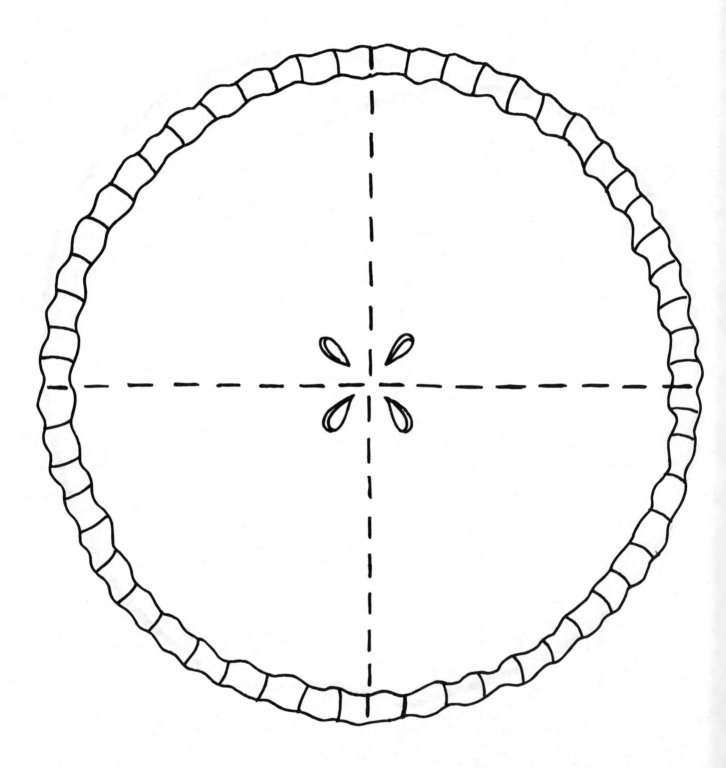

Peter, Peter, Pumpkin Eater

Peter, Peter, pumpkin-eater,
Had a wife and couldn't keep her;
He put her in a pumpkin shell,
And there he kept her very well.

Peter, Peter, Pumpkin Eater

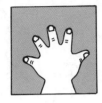

Pass the Pumpkin

Materials
small pumpkin or orange

Mother Goose in the garden.

Play this version of the game *Hot Potato* with a mini-pumpkin or orange. Invite students to sit in a circle. Have them pass around the pumpkin or orange as they recite the rhyme "Peter, Peter, Pumpkin Eater." Explain that the person holding the pumpkin or orange on the last word (*well*) must stand and say a word that rhymes with it. For example, *tell, sell,* or *bell.* Ask the student to sit back down, and repeat the process. When all the words that rhyme with *well* have been said, choose another word from the verse, such as *had, eat, keep,* or *he,* and then play the game again.

Harvest Mural

Materials
butcher paper
crayons or markers

Tell students that they are going to plan a harvest party for Peter and his wife. Explain to students that they are going to draw a mural that shows the feast. Organize students into small groups, and give each a large piece of butcher paper. Invite groups to draw pictures of things they know are available during the fall harvest, such as corn, sweet potatoes, squash, beans, and pumpkins. Encourage students to feature Peter, his wife, and their pumpkin shell in their mural. Invite each group to share their work with the rest of the class.

Pumpkin Products

Materials
Pumpkin activity page (page 46)
crayons or colored pencils
old magazines
scissors
glue

Invite students to list products that come from pumpkins, such as pie, seeds, bread, or pudding. Give each student a copy of the Pumpkin activity page, and ask him or her to draw a picture of these pumpkin treats in the pumpkin shell. Children can also cut pictures from magazines and glue them onto the activity pages. Display student work around the room.

Other Shells

Materials
chart paper/marker
drawing paper
crayons or markers
bookbinding materials

Invite students to make a list of things that have shells, such as a crab, oyster, turtle, armadillo, coconut, or peanut. Write students' ideas on chart paper. Invite each student to choose one object from the list, and have him or her write or dictate its name on the bottom of a piece of paper. Encourage students to draw pictures of their shelled objects above their words. Collect students' papers, and bind them together into a class book titled *A Dictionary That Tells of Shells*.

Pumpkin Problems

Materials
Pumpkin activity page (page 46)
pumpkin seeds or white beans
markers and crayons
glue
pencils

Give each student ten pumpkin seeds or beans and a copy of the Pumpkin activity page. Tell students to color their pumpkins one color and one side of each seed or bean another color. Invite students to show addition problems on their pumpkins using seeds or beans. Have students place all ten seeds or beans on the pumpkins with the white sides facing up. Ask students to turn any number of seeds or beans over to reveal the colored side. Have them glue their seeds or beans to their pumpkins and write out the addition problems represented. Encourage students to share their work with classmates.

Pumpkin Notes

Materials
pumpkin seeds
plastic and/or metal containers with lids

Challenge students to think of creative ways to use their pumpkin seeds to make music. Students could place their seeds in a plastic container with a lid and shake it, or they could drop the seeds into a metal container or onto different surfaces. Invite students to use these music-making methods to create a melody for "Peter, Peter, Pumpkin Eater."

Living in a Pumpkin Shell

Materials
chart paper
marker

Ask students to brainstorm a list of animals. Write their ideas on chart paper. Read the name of an animal from the list, and ask the class to decide whether or not that animal would fit inside a pumpkin shell. If students say the animal *couldn't* fit inside a pumpkin shell, challenge them to think of another place this animal could fit.

Pumpkin Seed Sort

Materials
pumpkin seeds
magnifying glasses (one for each student pair)
paper

Divide the class into pairs. Give each pair ten pumpkin seeds, a magnifying glass, and two pieces of paper. Have students use the paper as work mats. Encourage them to use the magnifying glasses to examine and sort the pumpkin seeds into groups (for example, by size, color, shape, and so on). Invite students to share with the class how they sorted their seeds.

Name _____

Pumpkin

© Fearon Teacher Aids FE211010

Rub-a-Dub-Dub

Rub-a-dub-dub,
Three men in a tub,
And who do you think they be?
The butcher, the baker, the candlestick maker,
They all set out to sea.

Rub-a-Dub-Dub

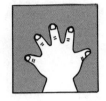

Hub-Person Says

Materials
none

Invite students to chant this version of "Rub-a-Dub-Dub" as they play a game similar to Simon Says. Have the class stand in a circle. Explain to students that a *hub* is the center of a circular object. Ask one student to stand in the hub of the circle and repeat an action, such as hopping on one leg or clapping. Invite the class to describe and imitate this action with the chant:

Mother Goose in the bathroom.

> *Rub-a-dub-dub,*
> *A person in the hub,*
> *What do you think she'll do?*
> *She's tapping her head*
> *Yes, tapping her head.*
> *Let's do the same thing, too.*

Invite a different student to perform a new action, and have the class repeat the process.

Meats Versus Sweets

Materials
sentence strips
marker
chalkboard/chalk
tape

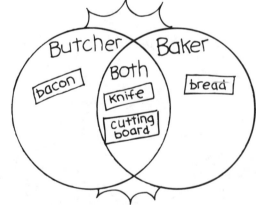

Print a list of food-related words, such as *hamburger, bread, pie, cake, knife, salt*, and *cutting board* on separate sentence strips. This activity could also be done with pictures instead of words. Draw a large Venn diagram (two interlocking circles) on the chalkboard, and label each circle *Butcher* or *Baker*. Hold up a strip, and ask students to decide if this word describes something related to a butcher, a baker, or both. Tape the strip to the appropriate place on the diagram. Encourage students to add their own words to the diagram. Repeat the activity with the butcher, baker, and candlestick maker.

48

Tub Toys

Materials
Tub activity page (page 52)
pencils
old magazines
scissors
glue
bookbinding materials

Give students copies of the Tub activity page, and have them write their names at the top. Encourage students to find pictures in magazines of toys they would like to take with them into the tub when they take a bath. Tell them to cut out the pictures and glue them to the tub. Collect students papers, and bind them into a class book titled *Tub Toys*.

Three Words in a Tub

Materials
chart paper
marker

Ask students to think of words that are described in the following version of the verse "Rub-a-Dub-Dub":

Rub-a-dub-dub,
Three words in a tub.
What do you think they be?
They each have three letters
And end with a t.
Please name them all for me.

Encourage students to name as many words as they can, while you write the words on chart paper. Change the underlined words, and repeat the activity.

Sink or Float?

Materials
Sink or Float? activity page (page 53)
bowls of water
two-liter plastic bottle caps
sponges
pennies
cottonballs
marbles
plastic spoons
pencils
paper towels

Give each student a copy of the Sink or Float? activity page. Organize students into groups of three or four. Distribute a bowl of water, two-liter bottle cap, sponge, penny, cottonball, marble, and plastic spoon to each group. Explain to students that they are going to place each object in the water to see whether it will sink or float. Ask students to predict which objects will sink and which ones will float. Tell children to record their predictions on the paper, circling the word *sink* or *float* beside each object's name. Have students take turns placing the objects in the bowl of water. Then ask them to record the actual results for each object beside their original predictions. Encourage groups to share their results with the class.

Tub Tunes

Materials
tub toys
empty plastic reclosable bottles
water

Invite students to bring squeeze toys to class, or have them fill plastic reclosable bottles with water. Encourage students to squeak or splash out a rhythm for the rhyme "Rub-a-Dub-Dub" using their tub-related musical instruments.

Tools of the Trade

Materials
Tools activity page (page 54)
pencils

Tell students that each of the three men in the verse "Rub-a-Dub-Dub" have lost an item they need to use in their jobs. Give each student a Tools activity page, and invite him or her to follow the maze to match each man with his tool.

Bubbles

Materials
bubble soap or dish soap
items for making bubbles (paper clip, drinking straw, handle of safety scissors)
shallow bowls or pans

Divide the class into several small groups. Give each group a shallow bowl containing approximately one inch (2.5 cm) of bubble soap. Encourage children to find objects to use as bubble wands for blowing bubbles. Invite each group to choose their favorite bubble wand to share with the class. Discuss what makes a good bubble wand.

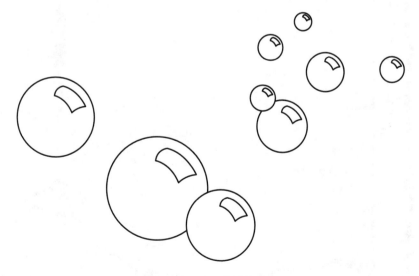

© Fearon Teacher Aids FE211010

Name _____

Tub

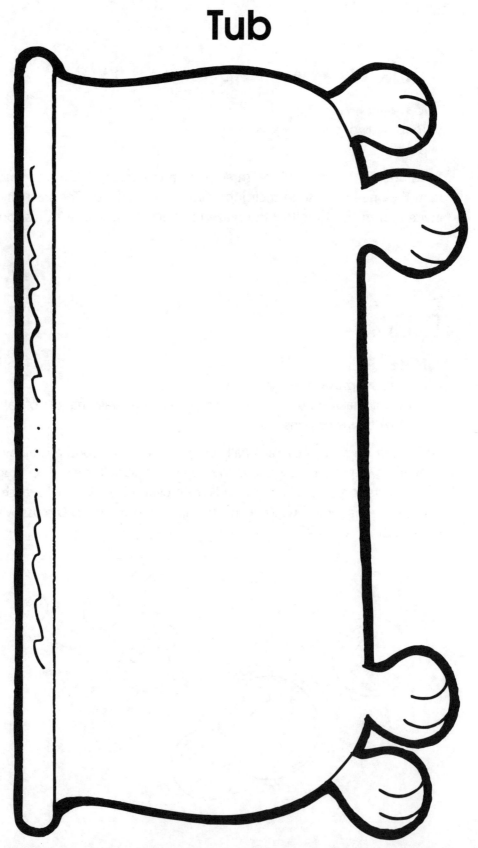

Sink or Float?

Object	Prediction	Actual
bottle cap	sink float	sink float
sponge	sink float	sink float
penny	sink float	sink float
cottonball	sink float	sink float
marble	sink float	sink float
plastic spoon	sink float	sink float

53

Tools

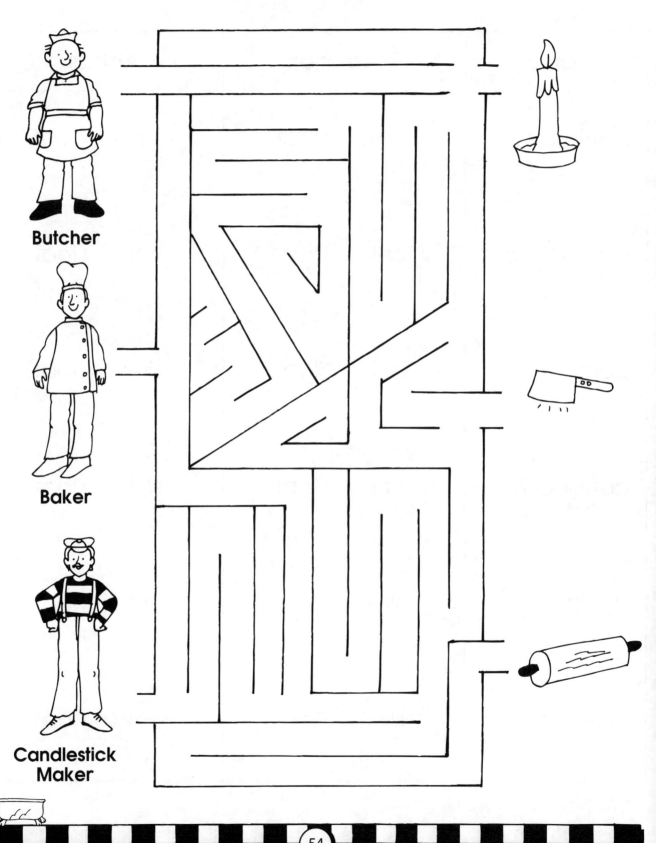

Butcher

Baker

**Candlestick
Maker**

© Fearon Teacher Aids FE21101

Twinkle, Twinkle, Little Star

Twinkle, twinkle, little star,
How I wonder what you are!
Up above the world so high,
Like a diamond in the sky.

When the blazing sun has set,
Then you show your little light.
Twinkle, twinkle, little star,
Twinkle, twinkle, all the night.

55

Twinkle, Twinkle, Little Star

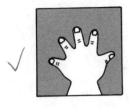

Star Match

Materials
none

Invite students to play this version of Mother, May I? Choose one student to be Little Star. Tell the rest of the class to stand at a distance from Little Star. Choose one student from the group to ask Little Star:

Twinkle, twinkle, little star,
May we take <u>three</u> steps to where you are?

Little Star should answer, *Yes, you may*, or *No, you may not. You may take <u>two</u> steps.* Invite students to change the underlined part of the sentences, and repeat the process. Play until a student reaches Little Star.

Mother Goose in the bedroom.

discussion only

You're a Star!

Materials
Star activity page (page 60)
pencils
crayons or colored pencils

Make one copy of the Star activity page. Write *You're a Star!* along the bottom of the page. Make one copy of the revised activity page for each student. Pair students together. Encourage pairs to talk with each other to learn something special that they each can do. Ask students to write their partners' names at the tops of the stars, and have them draw pictures of the special things their partners can do in the space below. Invite students to share what they learned about their partners with the class.

Wonderful Wishes

Materials
Wish activity page (page 61)
pencils
crayons or colored pencils

Distribute a copy of the Wish activity page to each student. Invite students to read aloud the poem "Star Light, Star Bright." Ask students to think about a wish they have, and invite them to record it in the space beside the poem. Encourage them to illustrate their pages as well. Display student work around the room.

Star Words

Materials
chart paper
markers
butcher paper

This is a jar full of stars.

Invite students to name words that rhyme with *star*, such as *far*, *car*, and *jar*, and write the words on chart paper. Organize the class into small groups. Give each group a piece of butcher paper, and assign them a rhyming word. Ask each group to draw a mural that shows the rhyming word interacting with a star or stars. Have each group write or dictate a sentence that includes the rhyming word and the word *star* along the bottom of their paper. For example, the group that has the word *car* might draw a car that is decorated with stars and driving along a road above the sentence *This car has stars*. Or, a group with the word *jar* might draw a large jar that is filled with stars above the sentence *This is a jar full of stars*. Display student work around the room.

Star Graph

Materials
Star activity page (page 60)
Graph activity page (page 16)
marker
scissors
crayons or colored pencils
construction paper, various colors

Make a copy of the Graph activity page.
Write one color word (*blue, yellow, green,*
and *pink*) in each box along the bottom.
Make one copy of the revised Graph activity
page for each student. Organize the class
into small groups. Make a copy of the Star
activity page for each group. Tell students to
cut out their stars and use them to trace and cut five blue, four yellow, three green,
and two pink stars (substitute colors if necessary) from construction paper.
Encourage students to determine how many stars of each color they have, and have
them record the information by coloring the corresponding number of boxes on
their Graph pages. Encourage groups to compare their work.

Easy as ABC

Materials
none

Invite the class to sing and compare the melodies of the songs "Twinkle, Twinkle,
Little Star" and "The ABC Song." Organize the class into two groups and assign one
song to each group. Invite both groups to sing their songs at the same time. Extend
the activity by dividing the class into smaller groups, and have them sing one or
both songs as a round.

Star Shapes

Materials
star stickers
black construction paper
white crayons

Discuss with students how stars in the sky form pictures. Give each student some star stickers and a piece of black construction paper. Encourage students to randomly place the stickers on their paper. Then have them use a white crayon to connect their stars to create a picture. Invite volunteers to explain their star pictures to the class.

Star Search

Materials
chalkboard/chalk

Explain that at night we can see many stars in the sky, but during the day we can only see one very bright star—the sun. Invite children to look at the sky and observe where the sun is in the sky in the morning, at noon, and at the end of the school day. (Make sure children are careful to never look directly at the sun.) Record children's observations on the chalkboard. Discuss what happens to the sun.

Explain that the stars, sun, and moon appear to move in the sky throughout the day and night, but it is the earth that is actually moving and the sun, stars, and moon that remain in the same place.

Name _____

Star

Name _____

Wish

Star light, star bright,
The first star I see tonight.
I wish I may, I wish I might
Have the wish I wish tonight.

Hey, Diddle, Diddle

Hey, diddle, diddle!
The cat and the fiddle,
The cow jumped over the moon;
The little dog laughed
To see such sport,
And the dish ran away with the spoon.

© Fearon Teacher Aids FE211010

Hey, Diddle, Diddle

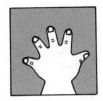

Moon Tune

Materials
"Hey, Diddle, Diddle" verse (page 62)
Cow activity page (page 67)
Moon activity page (page 68)
Dog activity page (page 31)
Dish activity page (page 69)
Spoon activity page (page 70)
crayons or markers
scissors

Mother Goose on the porch.

Organize the class into small groups, and give each student a copy of the "Hey Diddle, Diddle" verse and the Cow, Moon, Dog, Dish, and Spoon activity pages to color and cut out. Tell each group to change the underlined parts of the verse and use their cutouts to demonstrate the actions. For example, a group might create the following verse:

> Hey diddle, diddle,
> The cat and the fiddle.
> The cow _jumped under_ the moon.
> The little dog _cried_
> To see such sport.
> And the dish _danced around_ with the spoon.

Encourage each group to perform their new verses and actions for the rest of the class.

Mirror Mates

Materials
Cat activity page (page 71)
Fiddle activity page (page 72)
Cow activity page (page 67)
scissors

Moon activity page (page 68)
Dish activity page (page 69)
Spoon activity page (page 70)

Copy and have students cut out the figures on the Cat, Fiddle, Cow, Moon, Dish, and Spoon activity pages. Tell students that the verse "Hey, Diddle, Diddle" is filled with pairs. Prompt students to see that the cat and fiddle, cow and moon, and dish and spoon are paired together. Organize the class into a circle and randomly scatter the six cutouts amongst six students. Tell students that they will recite the verse "Hey, Diddle, Diddle." When students say *The cat*, have the student holding the cat cutout stand and perform an action, for example, hopping or tapping toes. Explain that the student holding the cutout that is paired with the cat (the fiddle) should imitate the action of the first student. Tell the cow and moon and dish and spoon to follow the same procedure when their names are called in the verse. (There should be six students performing three different actions by the end of the verse.) At the end of the verse, ask the six students to pass their cutouts to the people sitting to the right of them. Invite the class to repeat the procedure. Play until each student has had at least one chance to hold a cutout.

If I Could Be . . .

Materials
Cat activity page (page 71)
Fiddle activity page (page 72)
Cow activity page (page 67)
Moon activity page (page 68)
crayons or markers
glue

Dog activity page (page 31)
Dish activity page (page 69)
Spoon activity page (page 70)
pencils
scissors
construction paper

Make several copies of the Cat, Fiddle, Cow, Moon, Dog, Dish, and Spoon activity pages available to students. Invite students to decide which of these characters they would like to be, and have them write or draw their reasons on a copy of that character. Encourage students to color, cut out, and glue their work onto a piece of construction paper before sharing it with the rest of the class.

Cow Jumps Over Moon

Materials

chart paper

As a class, have students dictate a newspaper article about the cow who jumped over the moon. Write students' ideas on chart paper. Be sure to include the answers to the questions *who, what, when, where*, and *why* in the newspaper article.

Lunar Leap

Materials

Cow activity page (page 67)
masking tape
pencils

Give each student a copy of the Cow activity page. Ask students to write their names on the cows and cut them out. Lead students and their cow cutouts to a large open area. Pair students together, and give each pair some masking tape. Have one student place a piece of tape on the ground to mark the place where she or he will start jumping. Have the student jump as far as he or she can, and mark the length of the jump with a piece of tape. Ask the jumper's partner to use the cow cutouts to measure how far the student jumped. Record the length of the jump on the back of the jumper's cow cutout. Then students switch places and repeat the activity.

Milk for Sale

Materials

Explain to students that a "jingle" is a short, catchy tune that is written to sell a product. Invite students to sing television and radio jingles that they know. Tell students that they have been "hired" to write a jingle to sell the special milk produced by the cow that jumped over the moon. Encourage groups to perform their jingles for the class.

Fearon Teacher Aids FE211010

These Murals Are Quite a Sight

Materials

Cat activity page (page 71)
Fiddle activity page (page 72)
Cow activity page (page 67)
Moon activity page (page 68)
butcher paper

Dog activity page (page 31)
Dish activity page (page 69)
Spoon activity page (page 70)
crayons or markers
paint/paintbrushes

Organize the class into small groups. Distribute to each group a copy of the Cat, Fiddle, Cow, Moon, Dog, Dish, and Spoon activity pages to color and cut out. Give each group a large piece of butcher paper, paint, and paintbrushes, and invite them to create a backdrop for their characters. Encourage students to use their murals and character cutouts to tell the story of "Hey, Diddle, Diddle."

Animal Movements

Materials

This activity engages children's knowledge of animal movements, as well as their listening skills. Explain that in the rhyme "Hey, Diddle, Diddle" the animal movements are very unusual. Ask students to describe what the animals are doing. As a class, think of movements from the rhyme that children can do and remember easily. Include other animal movements, too. Then have them practice the movements, following your example.
Some movements might include:

> A cow jumping. (Jump up and down in place.)
> A cat fiddling. (One arm holds the "fiddle" while the other arm moves back and forth pretending to play it.)
>
> A bird flying. (Flap arms up and down at sides.)
> A rabbit hopping. (With hands held at chest level, take short hops.)

When you say "cow jumping" to the class, they should all jump on cue until you tell them to stop. Next say something like "birds jumping." The class should remain motionless. Continue with all the animal movements. Have children take turns playing the role of the leader.

66

Name _____

Cow

© Fearon Teacher Aids FE211010

reproducible

Name _____

Moon

© Fearon Teacher Aids FE211010

Name _____

Dish

© Fearon Teacher Aids FE211010

reproducible

Spoon

© Fearon Teacher Aids FE21101

Name _____

Cat

reproducible

Name _____

Fiddle

One, Two, Buckle My Shoe

One, two, buckle my shoe;
Three, four, shut the door;
Five, six, pick up sticks;
Seven, eight, lay them straight;
Nine, ten, a big fat hen.

One, Two, Buckle My Shoe

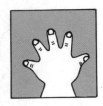

Stepping Out

Materials
Shoe activity page (page 14)
crayons or markers
scissors

Organize students into small groups, and lead them to a large open area. Give each group several copies of the Shoe activity page to color and cut out. Invite each group to lay a path with their shoe cutouts for another group to follow.

Mother Goose goes out the door.

One, Two, Do Something New

Materials
none

Invite the class to sit in a circle. Ask one student to go to the center of the circle. Teach the class the following version of "One, Two, Buckle My Shoe," and encourage the student in the center of the circle to pantomime an action:

Verse	Sample Actions
One, two, do something new.	Student hops.
Three, four, do it some more.	Student continues hopping.
Five, six, well do your tricks.	Class hops along with student.
Seven, eight, that was great.	Class claps for student.
Nine, ten, let's do it again.	Class hops again.

Invite a different student to go to the center of the circle. Ask the class to repeat the verse, and encourage the new student to try a new action.

One, Two, Do I Know You?

Materials
Door activity page (page 78)
pencils
scissors
glue
white construction paper
crayons or markers

Make one copy of the Door activity page. Write the following couplets on the door: *One, two, heard what's new?/Three, four, open the door*. Give students revised copies of the Door activity page, and have them write their names at the top. Show students how to cut the door along the dotted lines. Have them glue the doorframe to white construction paper so that the door swings open. Invite students to draw something that has happened to them recently in the space behind the door. For example, the birth of a new sibling, a birthday, or a visit to the zoo. Encourage each student to meet with a partner. Tell one student to say to the other, *One, two, tell me what's new*. Have the partner respond, *Three, four, open the door*. Encourage the first student to name what is new in his or her partner's life. Then have students change places and repeat the activity.

Door Words

Materials
Door activity page (page 78)
pencils
scissors
glue
white construction paper

Organize students into small groups. Give each group a copy of the Door activity page. Assign each group a different word from the verse "One, Two, Buckle My Shoe," such as *shoe, door, stick, straight*, or *hen*. Have one member of each group write or dictate his or her word across the front of the door. Show students how to cut the door along the dotted lines, and have them glue the frame to white construction paper. (Behind the door, have each group list as many words or pictures as they can that rhyme with the word on the front.) Ask groups to share their rhyming-word lists before you post their work around the room.

One, Two, I'll Add for You

Materials

I'll Add for You activity pages (pages 79 and 80)
crayons or colored pencils
stapler
construction paper

Invite small groups of students to illustrate a new version of "One, Two, Buckle My Shoe." If possible, make a double-sided copy using both I'll Add for You activity pages. Then give each student a two-sided activity page. Have students draw each specified item the number of times indicated in the math sentences. Then have students add the number of objects together and write this number on the line provided. For example, in the first space, have students draw one thing that is blue and two things that are blue. Since one plus two equals three, students fill in the line to read *three things that are blue*. Encourage students to repeat the process with the remaining three sentences.

Musical Numbers

Materials

simple instrument (horns, triangles, dried beans
in empty film containers, drums)

Organize the class into five small groups. Give each group different simple instruments, such as horns, triangles, dried beans in empty film containers, or drums. Assign each group a pair of numbers from the verse "One, Two, Buckle My Shoe." Invite the class to say the verse, and ask each group to play their instruments when their numbers are called. Encourage each group to trade instruments with another group, and repeat the process.

76

Sewing Shoes

Materials
Shoe activity page (page 14)
crayons or markers
tagboard
scissors
hole punch
string or yarn

Distribute one copy of the Shoe activity page to each student. Invite students to color the shoes. Have them glue the shoes onto separate pieces of tagboard and cut them out. Help them use a hole punch to make holes around each shoe. Give each student a piece of string or yarn. Show students how to sew around their shoes. Invite interested students to try to explain how to tie a shoe.

Different Shoes

Materials
none

Divide the class into small groups. Have children in each group sit in a circle on the floor with their feet facing the center. Invite each child to take off his or her left shoe and place it in a pile in the center of the circle. Mix up the shoes. Ask a volunteer to choose a shoe from the pile and try to find the child with the matching shoe. Have another child choose a shoe and find its mate. Continue until all the children have their own shoes back. Discuss how each child could identify his or her own shoe.

77

Door

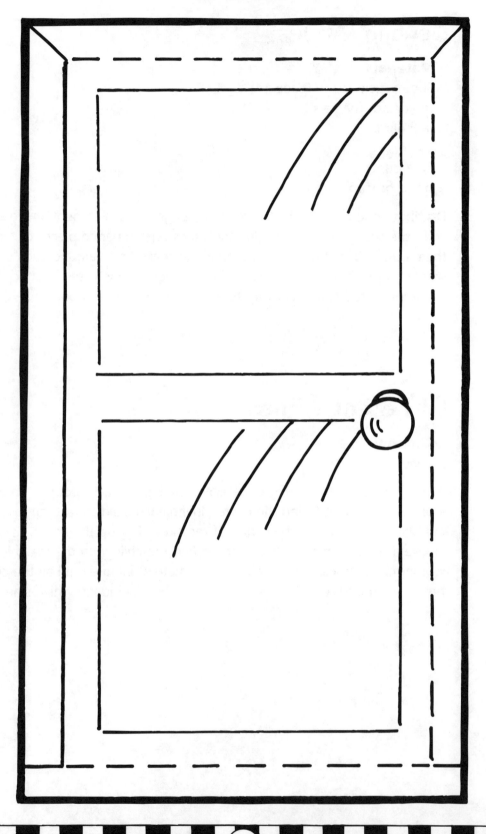

© Fearon Teacher Aids FE211010

Name _____

I'll Add for You

One + Two = _____ things that are blue.

Three + Four = _____ shirts I wore.

79

Name _____

I'll Add for You

Five + Six = _____ toys to fix.

Seven + Eight = _____ foods that are great.

© Fearon Teacher Aids FE211010

Little Boy Blue

Little Boy Blue,
Come, blow your horn!
The sheep's in the meadow,
The cow's in the corn.
Where's that little boy
Who looks after the sheep?
Under the haystack,
Fast asleep!

Z-Z-Z-Z-Z

Little Boy Blue

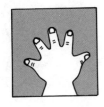

Clothing Color

Materials
none

This activity encourages students to practice naming colors and explore different body movements. Arrange students in a circle. Tell them to listen carefully for the name of a color. Explain that all students wearing that color should go to the middle of the circle and perform the activity that is named. Say the following version of Little Boy Blue to direct students' actions: *Little kids <u>red</u>,/Come <u>jump up and down</u>*. Change the underlined words and play again.

Mother Goose in the backyard.

Sheep to the Meadow, Cows to the Barn

Materials
none

Lead students to a large open area. Ask the class to stand on one side of the area, and invite one student to be Little Boy/Girl Blue. Whisper the word *cow* or *sheep* into the ear of each student. Have Little Boy/Girl Blue stand in the center of the play area, and prompt him or her to say, *Sheep in the meadow*. Tell all students who are "sheep" to run to the other side of the area. Encourage Little Boy/Girl Blue to tag as many students as possible. Students who are tagged become "haystacks," and must sit where they are tagged. Tell these students they should help Little Boy/Girl Blue tag the "cows" and "sheep" that run by. Have Little Boy/Girl Blue say, *Cows in the barn*. Tell "cows" to run across the area. Encourage Little Boy/Girl Blue to alternate between calling "sheep" and "cows" until each student has become a "haystack."

Farm Hands

Materials
Barn activity page (page 86)
chart paper
crayons or markers

Invite students to list jobs that people who live on farms have, such as milking cows, planting crops, and gathering eggs. Write students' ideas on chart paper. Give each student a copy of the Barn activity page. Encourage students to select one job from the list that they would like to do, and have them use words or pictures to describe this job on their activity pages.

Who's in the Meadow Now?

Materials
"Little Boy Blue" verse (page 81)
sentence strips
pocket chart
markers

Write the following version of "Little Boy Blue" on sentence strips. Use a different-colored sentence strip for the underlined words:

> Little boy blue,
> Come blow your horn.
> The <u>frog's</u> in the meadow
> The pig's in the corn.
> Where is that little boy
> Who looks after the <u>frog</u>?
> He's snoring away
> Under a <u>log</u>!

Invite students to change the underlined words, and invite them to recite and pantomime their new verses.

Missing Sheep

Materials
Missing Sheep activity page (page 87)
crayons or colored pencils
scissors
chalk/chalkboard

Distribute a copy of the Missing Sheep activity page to each student. Invite students to color and cut out their sheep. Have students place all five sheep in the meadow. Write a simple subtraction problem on the board, such as *5 – 1* or *5 – 3*. Encourage students to use their sheep to determine the answers to the problems. To extend the activity, have two students combine their sheep, and ask them to write subtraction problems with all ten animals.

Blow That Horn

Materials
paper-towel or toilet-tissue rolls
hole punch

Invite students to make horns from paper-towel or toilet-tissue rolls. Help them punch holes in their tubes in different places to create original sounds. Organize the class into small groups. Encourage each group to use their "horns" to create a melody for the verse "Little Boy Blue." Ask each group to perform their melody, and invite the other groups to imitate them.

84

Feeling Blue?

Materials
old magazines
scissors
glue
paper

Explain to students that the term *monochromatic* means "one color." Tell them that they are going to create a monochromatic collage (or collection of pictures that are one color) for the verse "Little Boy Blue." Have students look in magazines for pictures of things that are blue. Invite students to glue their pictures onto a piece of paper, and display student work under the title *Feeling Blue*.

Create a Mini-Meadow

Materials
alfalfa or clover-sprout seeds
cotton
clay
construction paper
scissors
jelly-roll pan
spray bottle with water

In this activity you will create a small edible "meadow." Spread the cotton across a jelly-roll pan. Dampen the cotton by spraying it with water. Sprinkle the seeds onto the cotton. Decorate the growing area with construction paper trees, haystacks, fences, sheep, and so on, to create a meadow scene. You can also use real rocks and twigs.

Place the mini-meadow in a sunny window. Make sure the seeds do not dry out. When seeds have formed small leaves and obtained a length of one to two inches (2.5 cm to 5 cm), "harvest" the sprouts. Add them to a tossed salad or egg salad served on crackers and enjoy with your class.

Fearon Teacher Aids FE211010

Name _____

Barn

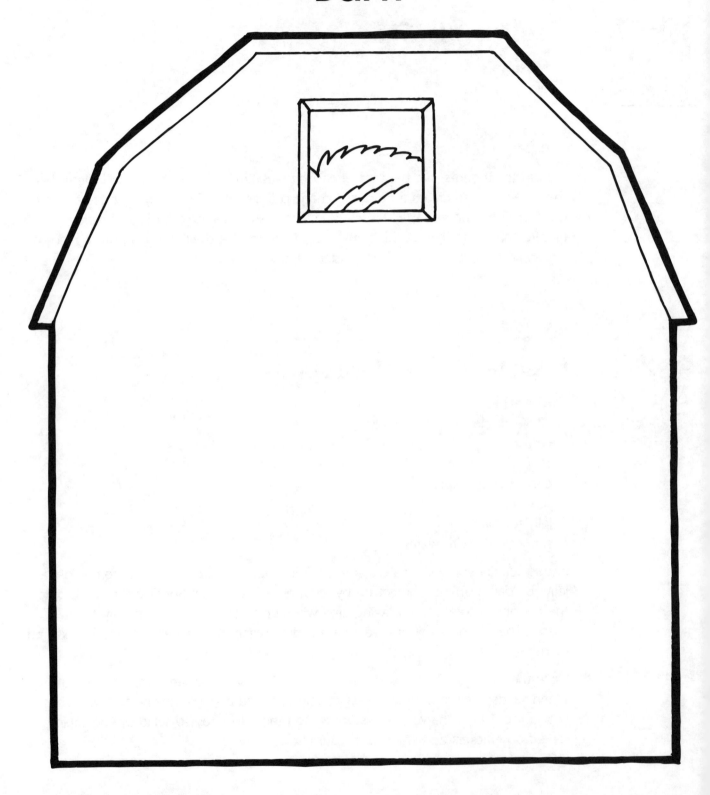

reproducible

Name _____

Missing Sheep

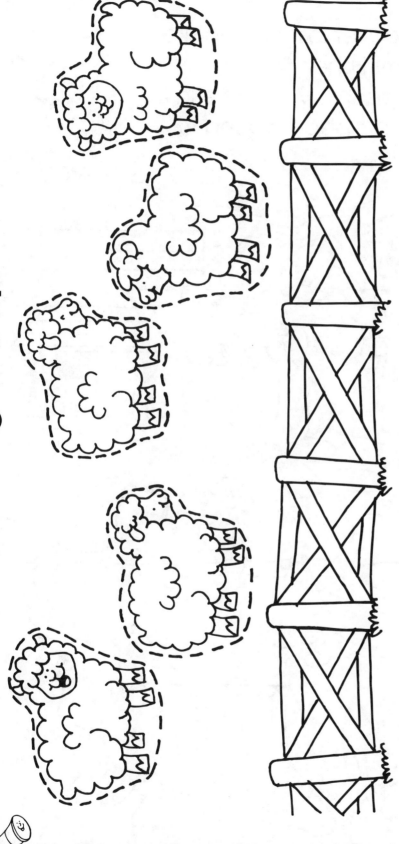

Lucy Locket

Lucy Locket lost her pocket,
Kitty Fisher found it;
Not a penny was there in it,
Just a ribbon 'round it.

reproducible

Lucy Locket

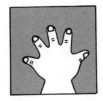

Putting Together a Pocket

Materials
Pocket activity page (page 93)
tagboard
pencils
scissors
hole punch
yarn
crayons or markers

Distribute copies of the Pocket activity page. Tell students to cut out the pocket, and have them trace it twice on a piece of tagboard. Ask students to cut out both pockets. Punch several holes around the perimeter of three sides of the pockets (excluding the topside). Give students pieces of yarn, and have them stitch both pockets together. Invite students to color both pockets and then tie a piece of string through the pockets' two top holes to create a strap.

What's in My Pocket?

Materials
Pocket activity page (page 93)
scissors
glue
crayons or markers
old magazines

Distribute two copies of the Pocket activity page to each student. Invite students to cut out both pockets and glue them together along the outer edges, excluding the top. (Students can also use the pocket they made in the previous activity.) Then have them cut out a magazine picture and place it inside their pockets. Ask students not to tell what their magazine pictures are.

Have students work with partners. Have one student ask her or his partner questions that require a *yes* or *no* answer to help guess the picture in his or her pocket. When the student names the picture correctly, partners switch places and repeat the activity.

What's in YOUR Pocket?

Materials
Pocket activity page (page 93)
Writing Lines activity page (page 24)
pencils
crayons or colored pencils
black marker

Make one copy of both the Pocket and Writing Lines activity pages. Cut out the pocket and trace the shape over the writing lines using a black marker. Make one copy of the lined pocket for each student. Invite students to think about something that they might keep in their pockets. Have each student draw a picture of this object on the front of the pocket. Then ask him or her to write or dictate about the object on the lines on the back of the pocket. Encourage children to read their stories to a partner.

Pocket Poetry

Materials
P-O-C-K-E-T Poem activity page (page 94)
pencils
crayons

Invite students to work with partners. Distribute a copy of P-O-C-K-E-T Poem activity page to each pair. Explain to students that they will write or dictate a poem about things that are found in pockets. Read aloud the first two sentences: *My pocket is very big you see. It holds my stuff from P to T.* Then have students write or dictate the name of an object that starts with each letter in the word *pocket*. For example, a student could write *pencil* or *paper clip* for the letter *p* and *olive* or *orchid* for the letter *o*. Display student work under the title *Pocket Poetry*.

Pocket Graph

Materials

Graph activity page (page 16)
index cards
chalkboard/chalk
tape
crayons or markers

Give each student an index card on which to write his or her name. Write the numerals *0, 1, 2, 3,* and *4+* along the bottom of the chalkboard. Invite students to tape their cards above the number that describes how many pockets they have in the clothes they are wearing today. Distribute a copy of the Graph activity page, and ask students to color the boxes that represent the number of students that have pockets. Ask students questions such as: *How many students are wearing clothes without pockets today? How many students are wearing an even number of pockets?*

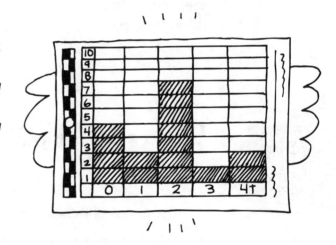

Pocket Music

Materials

unused, mismatched socks
yarn or string
various small objects (marbles, pennies, pebbles, keys, seashells)

Remind students that a pocket in the verse "Lucy Locket" is really a bag. Arrange students into small groups, and give each group several mismatched socks, yarn or string, and a quantity of small objects, such as marbles, pennies, pebbles, keys, and seashells. Have each group fill their socks with some of the objects they received. Show them how to tie a piece of string or yarn around the top of the sock to keep the objects secure. Encourage students to use their pockets to create musical accompaniment to a choral reading of the verse "Lucy Locket."

My Pocket Is Full!

Materials
Pocket activity page (page 93)
various small objects (marbles, pennies, pebbles, keys, seashells)

Invite students to work with partners. Give each pair of students a copy of the Pocket activity page and quantities of various small objects, such as marbles, pennies, pebbles, keys, and seashells. Ask one student to choose an object and predict how many will fit on the surface of the pocket. Have the other student determine the actual number that will fit. Encourage students to discuss the prediction and the actual results. Tell students to switch roles, and have them repeat the activity with a different object.

What's Missing?

Materials
tray
various small objects (crayon, marble, comb, whistle, seashell)

Have children sit in a circle. Explain that you have several objects in your pocket. For example, a crayon, comb, marble, and whistle. Pull the objects out of your pocket, place them on a tray, and show them to the class. Determine a set amount of time for children to look at the objects without touching them. Remove the objects from the room and take one item away from the tray. Return to the room with the tray, and ask children to guess which object is missing. The child who guesses correctly gets to go out in the hall to remove the next item.

Name _____

Pocket

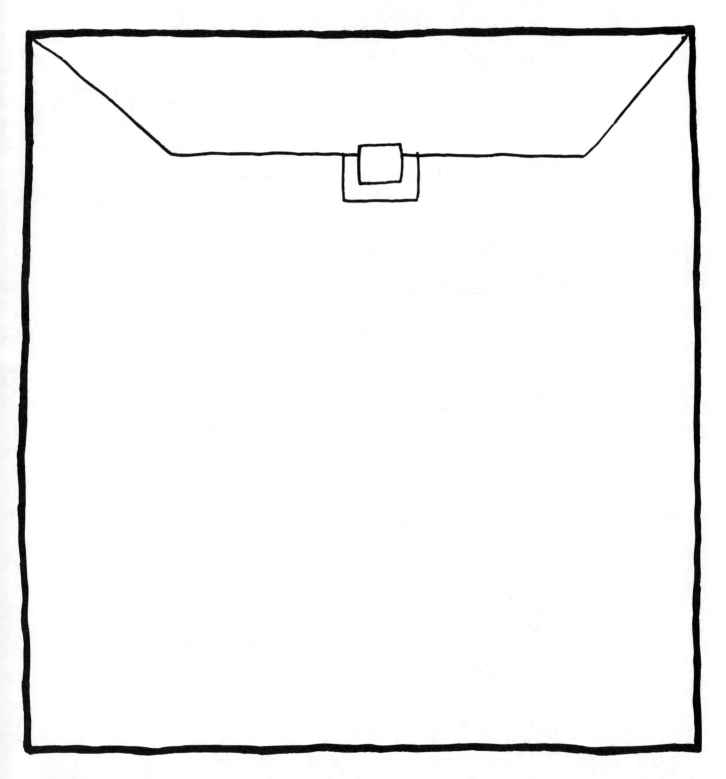

reproducible

P-O-C-K-E-T Poem

My pocket is very big you see.
It holds my stuff from P to T.

P _____

O _____

C _____

K _____

E _____

T _____

© Fearon Teacher Aids FE211010

Notes